READY, SET, CREATE!

WRITTEN BY
STEFFI CAVELL-CLARKE

Jobs in Art

KidHaven PUBLISHING

Published in 2027 by
KidHaven Publishing, an Imprint of Greenhaven Publishing, LLC
2544 Clinton St., Buffalo, NY 14224

Written by: Steffi Cavell-Clarke
Edited by: Noah Leatherland
Designed by: Ker Ker Lee

Cataloging-in-Publication Data
Names: Cavell-Clarke, Steffi.
Title: Jobs in art / Steffi Cavell-Clarke.
Description: Buffalo, NY : KidHaven Publishing, 2027. | Series: Ready, set, create! | Includes glossary and index.
Identifiers: ISBN 9781534570160 (pbk.) | ISBN 9781534570177 (library bound) | ISBN 9781534570184 (ebook)
Subjects: LCSH: Cultural industries--Vocational guidance--Juvenile literature. | Arts--Vocational guidance--Juvenile literature.
Classification: LCC HD9999.C9472 C349 2027 | DDC 700.23--dc23

Printed in China

CPSIA compliance information: Batch #QS27KH: For further information contact Greenhaven Publishing LLC at 1-844-317-7404.

Please visit our website, www.greenhavenpublishing.com. For a free color catalog of all our high-quality books, call toll free 1-844-317-7404 or fax 1-844-317-7405.

Find us on

Photo Credits – Images courtesy of Shutterstock.com, unless otherwise stated.

Cover & Recurring – Colorfuel Studio, DigitalShards, PeopleImages. 2–3 – Ermolaev Alexander. 4–5 – PeopleImages, Freedomz. 6–7 – wavebreakmedia, Trif. 8–9 – Tutatamafilm, Tanya_Terekhin. 10–11 – Dmytro Sheremeta, Andrew Angelov. 12–13 – Iryna Inshyna, Monkey Business Images. 14–15 – Pressmaster. 16–17 – Summit Art Creations, Lee Charlie. 18–19 – Monkey Business Images, NaMong Productions92. 20–21 – Frame Stock Footage, Kozlik. 22–23 – Lee Charlie, Prostock-studio.

Contents

Page 4 Working in the World of Art

Page 6 Painter

Page 8 Illustrator

Page 10 Photographer

Page 12 Art Teacher

Page 14 Curator

Page 16 Architect

Page 18 Fashion Designer

Page 20 Performing Arts

Page 22 Ready, Set, Create!

Page 24 Glossary and Index

WORDS THAT LOOK LIKE THIS CAN BE FOUND IN THE GLOSSARY ON PAGE 24.

Working in the World of Art

What would you like to be when you grow up? Do you love to paint, build, or sing? There are many different jobs in the world of art.

MAKING ART IS A GREAT WAY TO EXPRESS YOURSELF AND EXPLORE YOUR IMAGINATION.

The wonderful world of art is always growing and changing. Let's explore some of the jobs that help shape the art world of today. Maybe one will catch your eye!

Painter

A painter is an artist who uses paint to create pictures. Painting is a wonderful way to create something new for other people to see and enjoy.

Painters need to know how to mix colors. They use a paintbrush to create lines and shapes. They often work in a place where they feel inspired, such as a studio.

A STUDIO IS A ROOM WITH ART MATERIALS AND SPACE TO PAINT.

Illustrator

An illustrator is an artist who creates pictures to help bring a story to life. Their drawings help tell a story by showing you what the characters and places look like.

THESE DRAWINGS ARE CALLED ILLUSTRATIONS.

Illustrators use tools such as pencils, ink, and paint to create their illustrations. Some illustrators also use electronic tools to make art. You will often find their work in storybooks, comic books, and magazines.

Photographer

A photographer is an artist who takes photographs with a camera. Photographs capture a single, special moment in time, so you can remember it forever.

PHOTOGRAPHERS OFTEN TAKE PHOTOGRAPHS OF PEOPLE, ANIMALS, AND PLACES.

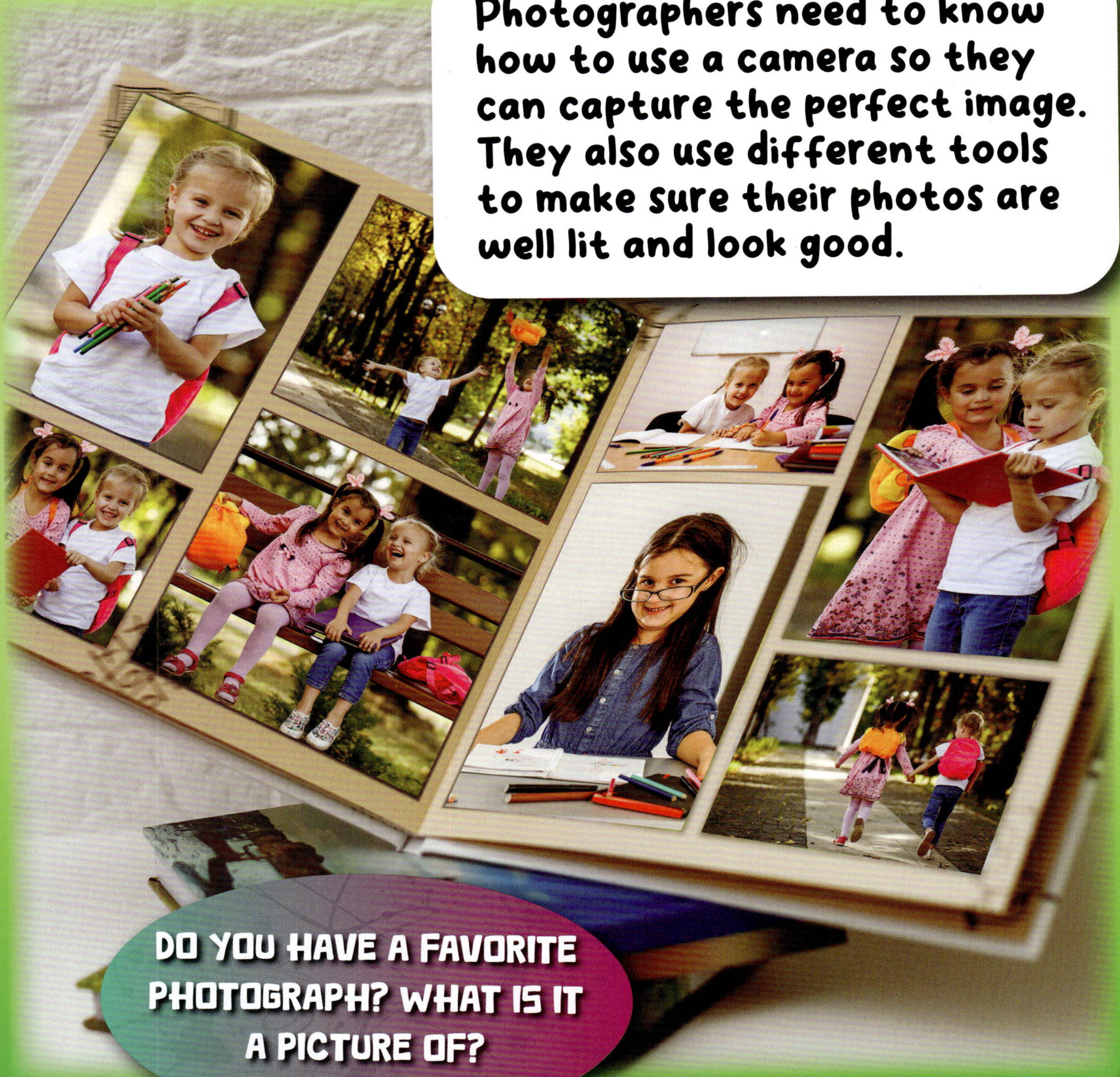

Photographers need to know how to use a camera so they can capture the perfect image. They also use different tools to make sure their photos are well lit and look good.

DO YOU HAVE A FAVORITE PHOTOGRAPH? WHAT IS IT A PICTURE OF?

Art Teacher

Art teachers help others learn all about art and help them improve their skills and techniques. They also help their students express their ideas and creativity in exciting new ways.

Art teachers often work in schools. They need to know about drawing, painting, sculpting, and many other forms of art. This helps them teach students how to express themselves in different ways.

Curator

A curator is someone who takes care of the artwork in a museum or gallery. They help choose how the art is displayed and make sure everything looks nice for the visitors.

Curators need to know about art, history, and the pieces they take care of. This helps them teach others about the stories, meanings, and history behind each piece.

Architect

Do you love to build and design interesting shapes? Then you may want to become an architect! An architect is someone who plans and designs buildings, such as houses and skyscrapers.

Architects help shape and build the world around us. They need to be good at problem solving, math, and planning. They use their creativity to design safe and useful buildings.

Fashion Designer

A fashion designer uses fabrics to create new clothes, shoes, and accessories. First, they usually sketch out a design. Then, they choose their fabrics and sew them together to make a new pattern and style.

Fashion designers need to know about lots of different types of fabrics. They need to be skilled at cutting, measuring, and sewing. Most of all, they need to love clothes and dressing up!

Performing Arts

The performing arts include different kinds of performances, such as singing, dancing, and acting. People all over the world enjoy watching performers share their amazing skills.

Performers need to practice often and work hard. They need to be brave and confident when showing their talents in front of others. It can be scary at first, but it gets easier with practice.

Ready, Set, Create!

The world of art is full of exciting jobs to discover. Each job is unique, but they all use creativity and skill to bring ideas to life and share them with others.

It can take a lot of practice and hard work to create something new. Whatever you want to be in life, keep working toward it, and watch your creativity and skills grow!

Glossary

fabrics	materials made by weaving threads of cotton, wool, nylon, silk, or other materials together
ink	a colored liquid used for writing, drawing, and printing
sculpting	making shapes by carving or molding materials
sketch	a quick, simple drawing with a pencil
students	people who are learning new things
techniques	ways of doing something

Index

buildings 16–17
cameras 10–11
clothes 18–19
history 15
museums 14
schools 13
students 12–13
studios 7
tools 9, 11